GUITAR ANTHOLOGY
GORDON LIGHTFOOT

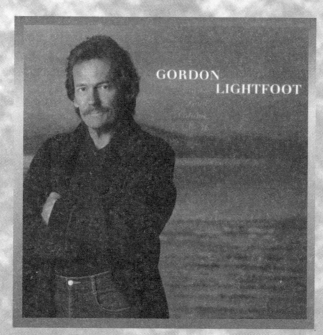

Transcribed by Hemme Luttjeboer

Editor: Aaron Stang
Music Editor: Colgan Bryan
Art Design: Joseph Klucar

CONTENTS

CANADIAN RAILROAD TRILOGY 6

CAREFREE HIGHWAY 3

CHRISTIAN ISLAND (Georgian Bay) 19

COLD ON THE SHOULDER 24

COTTON JENNY 38

EARLY MORNIN' RAIN 33

(That's What You Get)

FOR LOVIN' ME / DID SHE MENTION MY NAME 90

IF YOU COULD READ MY MIND 42

RAINY DAY PEOPLE 48

SOFTLY 53

SONG FOR A WINTER'S NIGHT (The Hands I Love) 58

STEEL RAIL BLUES 65

SUMMERTIME DREAM 72

SUNDOWN 76

THE WRECK OF THE EDMUND FITZGERALD 83

CAREFREE HIGHWAY

All gtrs. capo 2nd fret.

Words and Music by
GORDON LIGHTFOOT

Verse 2:
Turnin' back the pages to the times I love best,
I wonder if she'll ever do the same.
Now, the thing I call livin' is just bein' satisfied
With knowin' I got no one left to blame.

Verse 3:
Searchin' through the fragments of my dream shattered sleep,
I wonder if the years have closed her mind.
Well, I guess it must be wanderlust or tryin' to get free,
From the good old faithful feelin' we once knew.
(To Chorus:)

Chorus 2 & 4:
Carefree highway, I got to see you, my old flame.
Carefree highway, you seen better days.
The mornin' after blues, from my head down to my shoes;
Carefree highway, let me slip away,
Slip away on you.

CANADIAN RAILROAD TRILOGY

All gtrs. capo 3rd fret.
Gtr. 1 w/ "Drop D" tuning:
⑥ = D ③ = G
⑤ = A ② = B
④ = D ① = E

Words and Music by
GORDON LIGHTFOOT

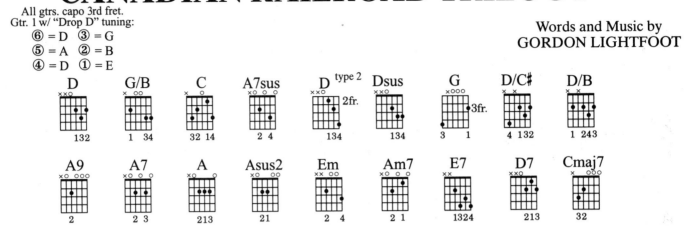

Moderately in 2 ♩ = 110

* **Gtr. 1** *(Acoustic 12-string)*

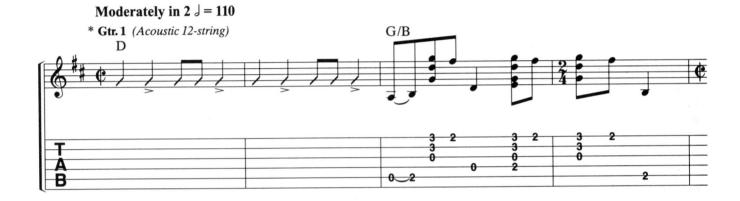

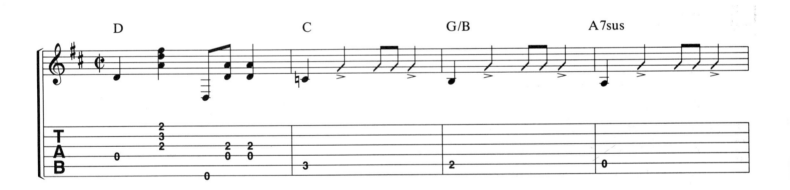

Canadian Railroad Trilogy - 13 - 1
PG9632

*Slide to 3rd ending only.

2. But time_
3. And when_

4. For they

Slightly slower ♩ = 106

Verse 4:

look in the fu - ture and what did they see?_____ They saw an

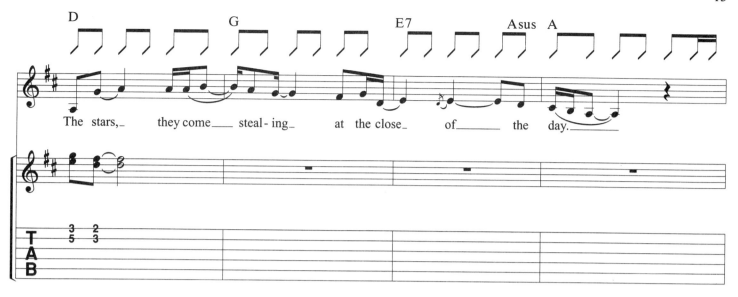

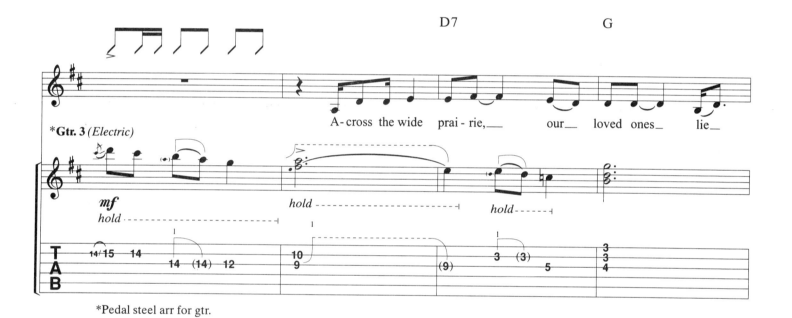

*Pedal steel arr for gtr.

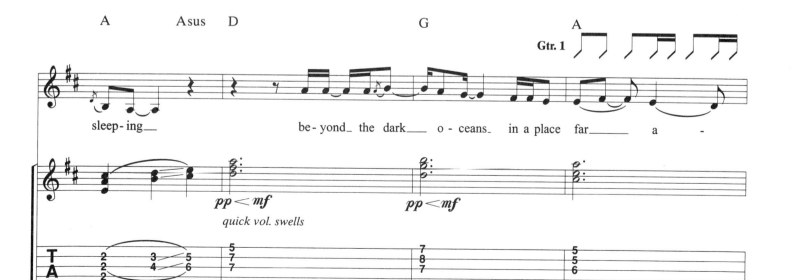

14

Faster ♩ 90 - 110
Verses 10 & 11:
w/Rhy. Fig. 1 *(Gtrs. 1 & 2) 2 times, simile*

10. So, o - ver the moun - tains and o - ver the plains.
11. *See additional lyrics*

In - to the Mus - keg and in - to the rain.

Up the Saint Law - rence, all the way to Gas - pé, we're

[1.] swing - ing out ham - mers and draw - ing our pay.

[2.] toast to the dead. 12. Our song

hold

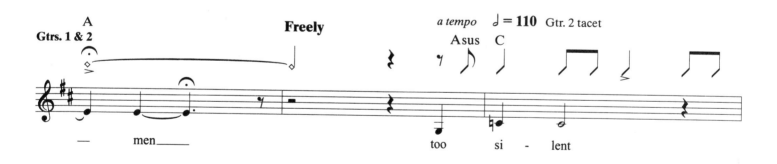

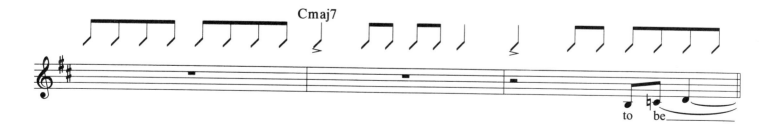

18

Outro:

Verse 2:
But time has no beginnings and history has no bounds,
As to this verdant country they came from all around.
They sailed upon her waterways and they walked the forests tall.
Built the mines, the mills and the factories for the good of us all.

Verse 3:
And when the young man's fancy had turned into the spring,
The railroad men grew restless for to hear the hammers ring.
Their minds were overflowing with the visions of their day,
With many a fortune won and lost and many a debt to pay.
(To Verse 4:)

Verse 11:
Drivin' 'em in and tyin' 'em down.
Away to the bunkhouse and into the town,
A dollar a day and a place for my head,
But a drink to the livin' and a toast to the dead.

CHRISTIAN ISLAND
(Georgian Bay)

All gtrs. capo at 2nd fret.

Words and Music by
GORDON LIGHTFOOT

Moderately ♩ = 110
Intro:

Gtr. 1 (Acoustic)

hold throughout

Gtr. 2 (Electric w/chorus)

Verses 1, 2 & 4:

sail - ing_ down to sum-mer wind._   I've got_ whisk-ers_ on my chin_
2.4. *See additional lyrics*

Rhy. Fig. 1

simile

hold --------------------

Christian Island - 5 - 1
PG9632

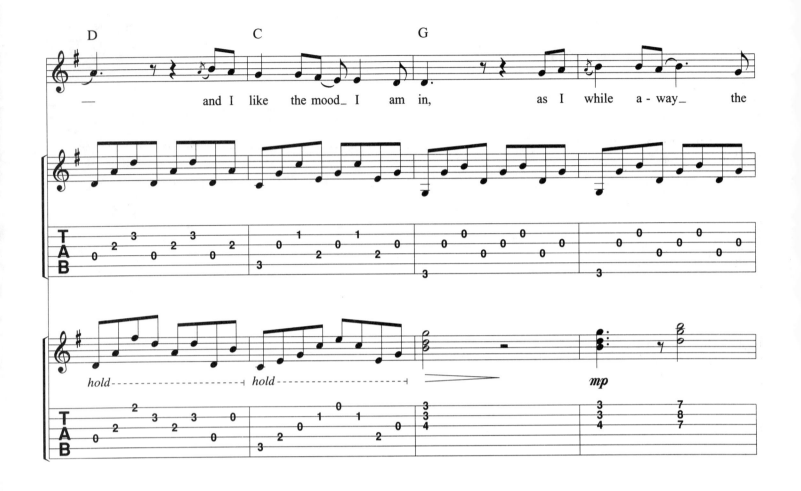

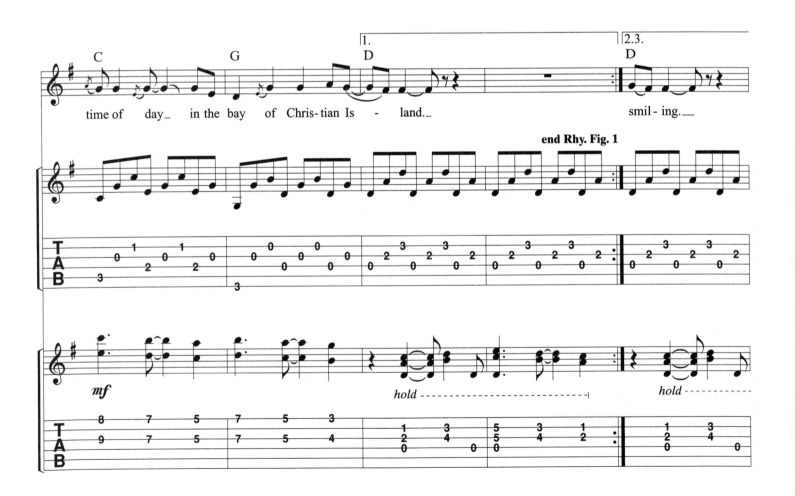

To Coda ⊕

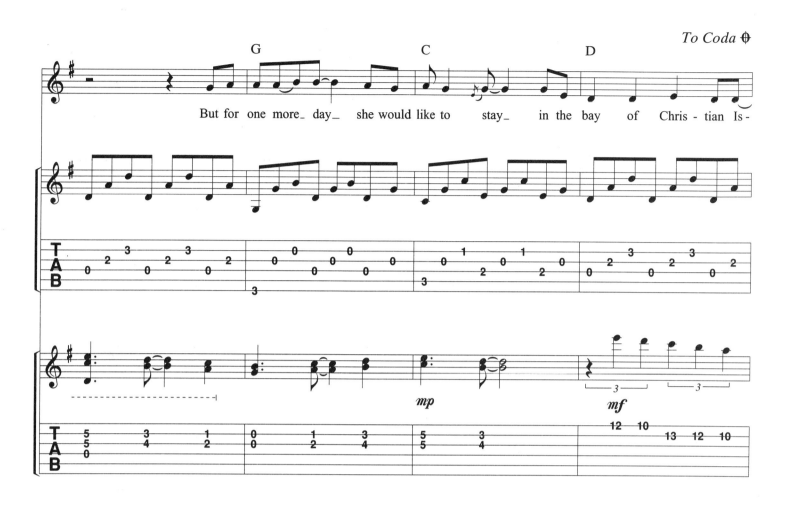

But for one more_ day_ she would like to stay_ in the bay of Chris - tian Is -

- land.

3. I'm

Gtr. 2

Gtrs. 2 & 3

Gtr. 3 *(Keybd. arranged for gtr.)*

Verse 2:
Tall and strong, she dips her rails.
I call her Silver Heels.
And she tells me how she feels.
She's a good old boat,
And she'll stay afloat
Through the toughest gale and keep smiling.
But for one more day she would like to stay,
In the bay of Christian Island.

Verse 4:
Tall and strong, she slips along.
I sing to her a song.
And she leans into the wind.
She's a good old boat,
And she'll stay afloat
Through the toughest gale and keep smiling.
When the summer ends we will rest again,
And we'll leave Christian Island.

COLD ON THE SHOULDER

All gtrs. capo 3rd fret.

Words and Music by
GORDON LIGHTFOOT

Moderately in 2 ♩ = 100

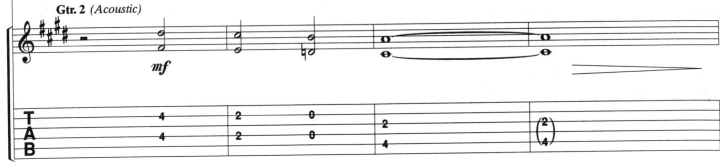

Give it a try,___ don't be rude;___

put it to the test and I'll give it right back to you.___

28

Cold on the Shoulder - 9 - 5
PG9632

30

Chorus:
w/Rhy. Fig. 2 *(Gtrs. 1 & 2) 2 times, simile*

cold___ on the shoul-der, and you know that we get a lit-tle, get a lit-tle old-er ev-'ry
Bkgd. vcl: Old - er ev - 'ry day.___

day. It's

cold___ on the shoul-der,_____ and you know that we get a lit-tle old-er ev-'ry day.___
Bkgd. vcl: Shoul-der.

To Coda ⊕

Gtr. 2

mf

Guitar Solo:

32

Coda

Outro:
w/Rhy. Fig. 2 (Gtrs. 1 & 2) simile

*On repeat.

Verse 4:
All I need is faith.
All we need is faith, faith, faith
To make it nice.
Kick it around, don't be rude.
If you're gonna make a mistake,
Don't you make it twice...

EARLY MORNIN' RAIN

All gtrs. capo 1st fret.

Words and Music by
GORDON LIGHTFOOT

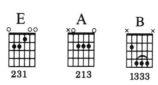

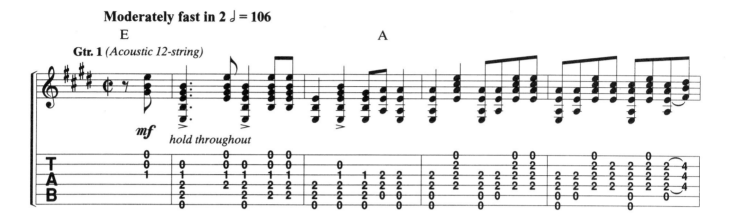

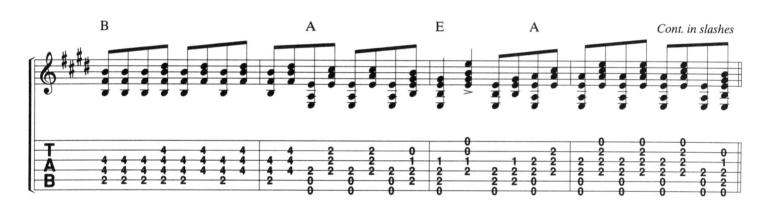

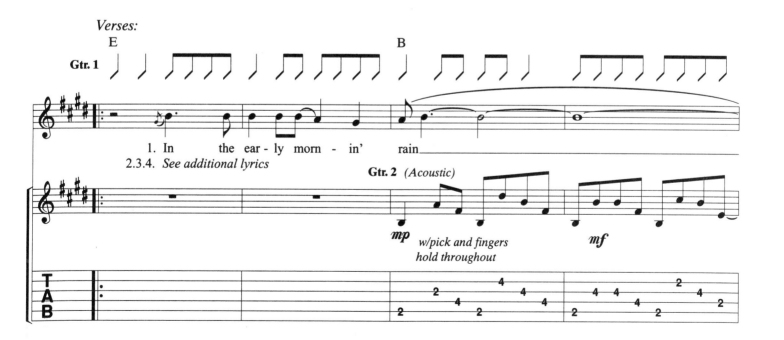

Verse 2:
Out on runway number nine,
Big 707 set to go,
But I'm stuck here in the grass
Where the pavement never grows.
Now, the liquor tasted good,
And the women all were fast,
Well, there she goes, my friend,
She'll be rollin' down at last.

Verse 3:
Hear the mighty engines roar,
See the silver bird on high,
She's away and westward bound,
Far above the clouds she'll fly
Where the mornin' rain don't fall
And the sun always shines,
She'll be flyin' over my home
In about three hours time.

Verse 5:
This old airport's got me down,
It's no earthly good to me,
And I'm stuck here on the ground
As cold and drunk as I can be.
You can't jump a jet plane
Like you can a freight train.
So, I'd best be on my way
In the early mornin' rain.

Early Mornin' Rain - 5 - 5
PG9632

COTTON JENNY

All gtrs. capo 2nd fret.

Words and Music by
GORDON LIGHTFOOT

Cotton Jenny - 4 - 2
PG9632

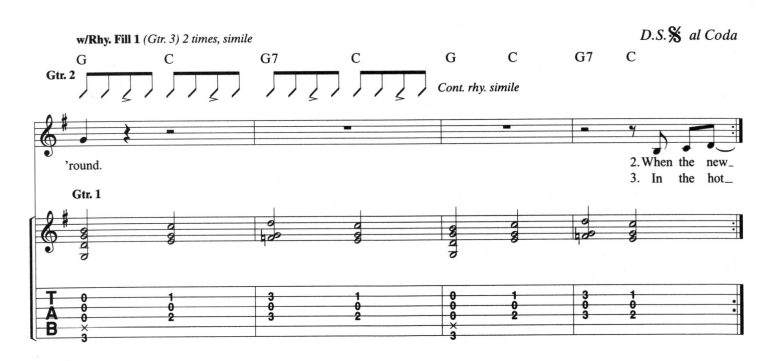

Outro:
w/Rhy. Fill 1 *(Gtr. 3) 4 times, simile*

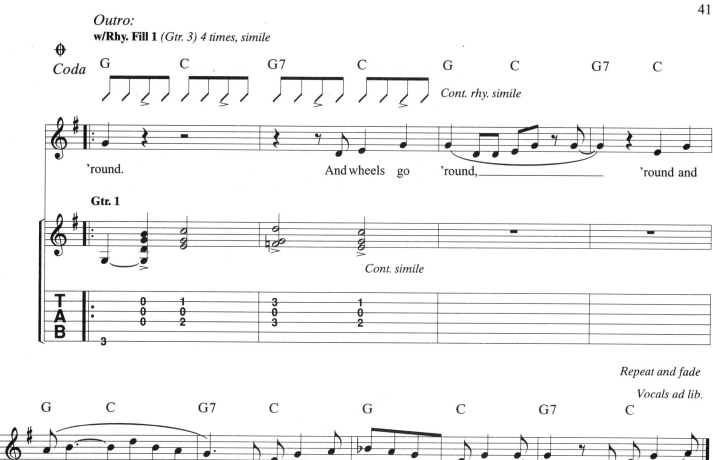

Repeat and fade
Vocals ad lib.

Verse 2:
When the new day begins,
I go down to the cotton gin
And I make my time worthwhile to them,
Then I climb back up again.
And she waits by the door,
"Oh, Cotton Jenny, I'm sore."
She rubs my feet while the sun goes down,
And the wheels of love go 'round.
(To Chorus:)

Verse 3:
In the hot, sickly south,
When they say, "Well, shut my mouth,"
I can never be free from the cotton grind.
But I know I got what's mine.
A soft, southern flame,
Oh, Cotton Jenny's her name.
She wakes me up when the sun goes down,
And the wheels of love go 'round.
(To Chorus:)

IF YOU COULD READ MY MIND

Gtr. 1 capo 2nd fret.

Words and Music by
GORDON LIGHTFOOT

Moderately fast ♩ = 120

Intro:

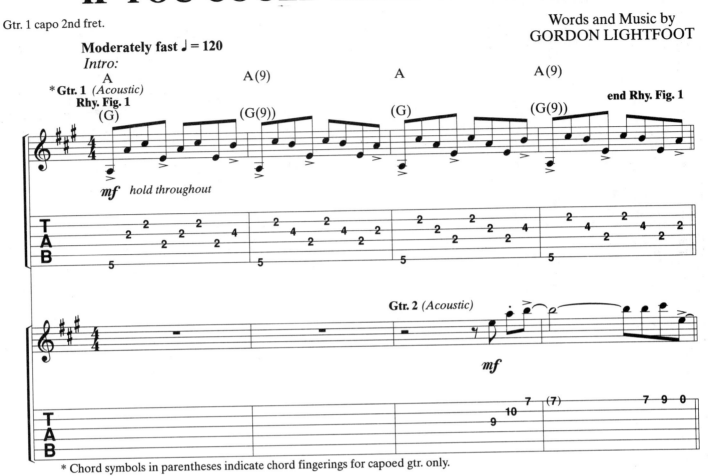

* Chord symbols in parentheses indicate chord fingerings for capoed gtr. only.

Verses:

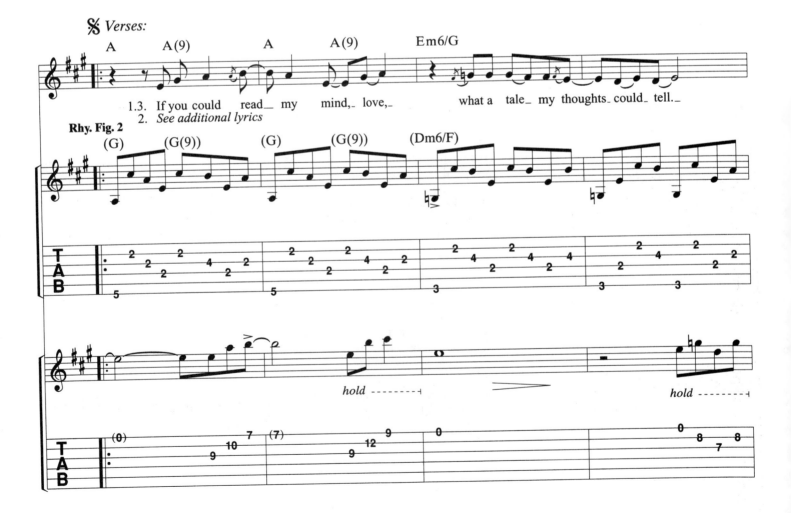

1.3. If you could read__ my mind,_ love,_ what a tale_ my thoughts_ could_ tell._
2. *See additional lyrics*

If You Could Read My Mind - 6 - 1
PG9632

If You Could Read My Mind- 6 - 2
PG9632

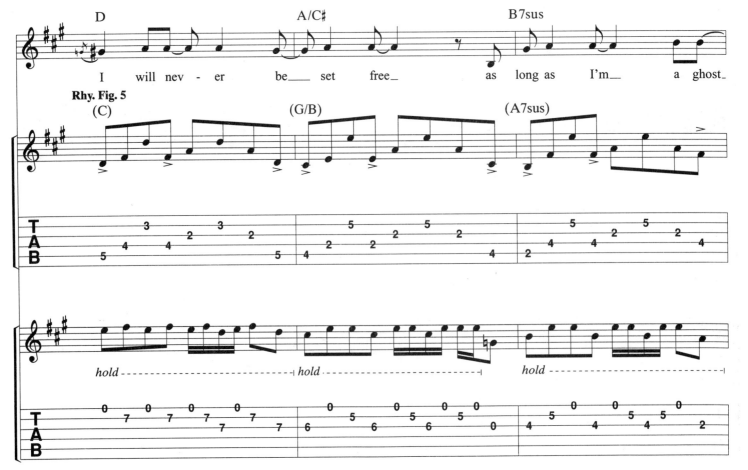

If You Could Read My Mind- 6 - 3

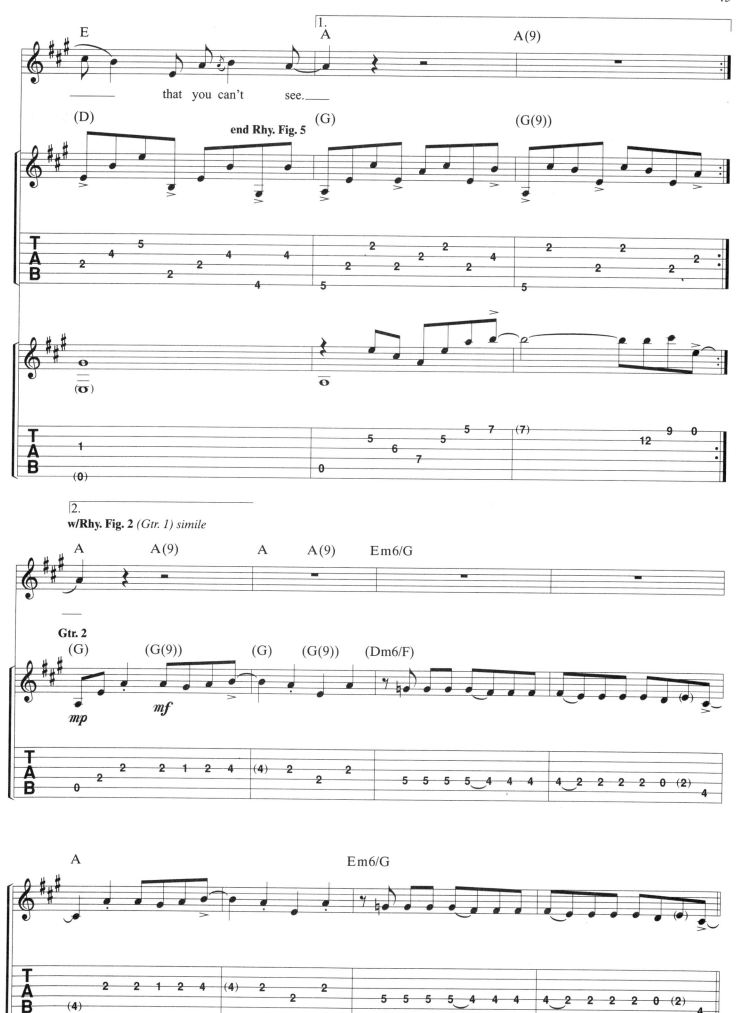

Verse 2:
If I could read your mind, love,
What a tale your thoughts could tell.
Just like a paperback novel,
The kind the drugstore sells.
When you reach the part where the heartaches come,
The hero would be me.
But heroes often fail.
And you won't read that book again
Because the ending's just too hard to take.

RAINY DAY PEOPLE

All gtrs. capo 2nd fret.

Words and Music by
GORDON LIGHTFOOT

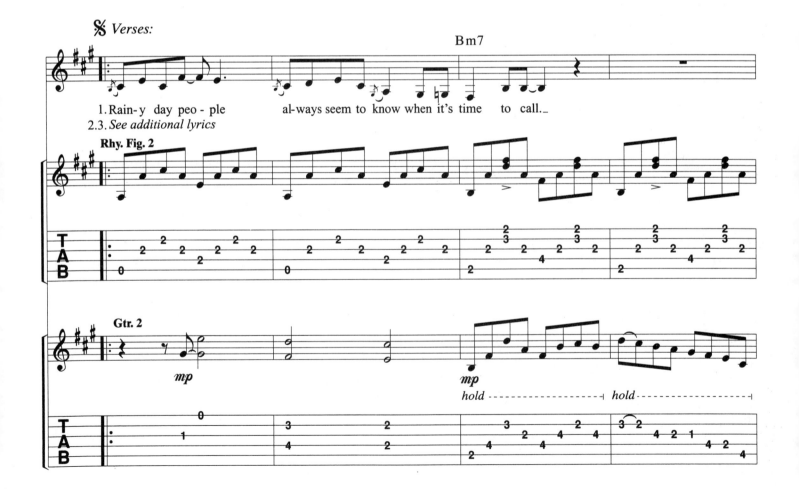

50

To Coda ⊕

rain - y day peo - ple don't_ mind if you're cry - in'____ a tear__ or two.__

end Rhy. Fig. 3

Gtr. 2

end Rhy. Fig. 3A

hold

Gtr. 3

1.

A

Enter pedal steel

2. w/Rhy. Fig. 2 (Gtr. 1) simile

A

Gtr. 2

mp

Gtr. 2

Gtr. 3

Gtr. 3

mp

Chorus:
w/Rhy. Figs. 3 and 3A *(Gtrs. 1, 2 & 3) simile*

Rain-y day lov-ers don't_ lie when they tell you_ they been down_ there,_ too.____

Rain-y day peo-ple don't_ mind if you're cry-in'____ a tear____ or two.____

w/Rhy. Figs. 1 & 1A *(Gtrs. 1, 2 & 3) simile*

D.S. 𝄋 al Coda

Rain- y day lov- ers don't_ hide love in - side, they just pass__ it on.__

Verse 2:
If you get lonely, all you really need is that rainy day love;
Rainy day people all know there's no sorrow they can't rise above.

Chorus:
Rainy day lovers don't love any others,
That would not be kind;
Rainy day people all know how it hangs
On your peace of mind.

Verse 3:
Rainy day people always seem to know when you're feelin' blue;
High-steppin' strutters who land in the gutter sometimes need one, too.

Chorus:
Take it or leave it, or try to believe it
If you been down too long;
Rainy day lovers don't hide love inside,
They just pass it on.

SOFTLY

All gtrs. capo 2nd fret.

Words and Music by
GORDON LIGHTFOOT

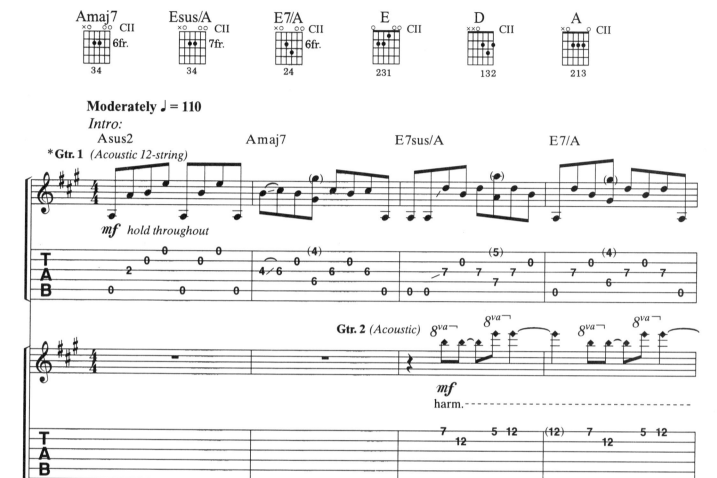

* 12-string written as 6-string gtr.
Notes in parentheses represents actual
pitch of 12-string gtr.

Softly - 5 - 1
PG9632

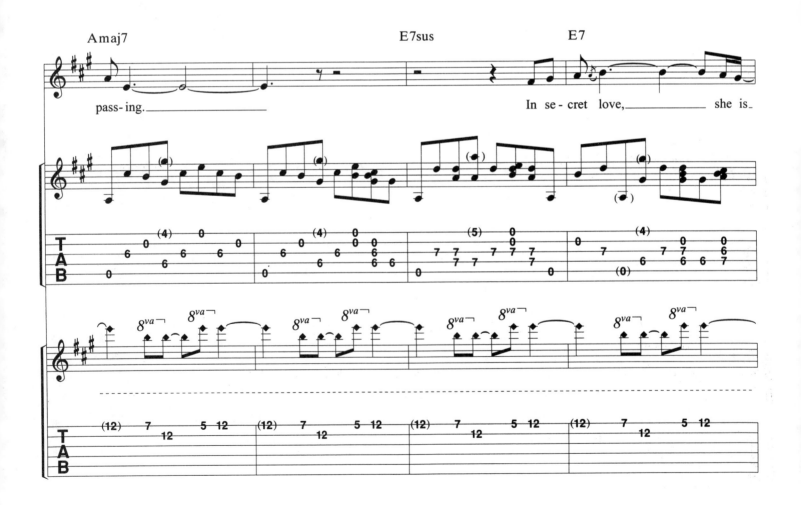

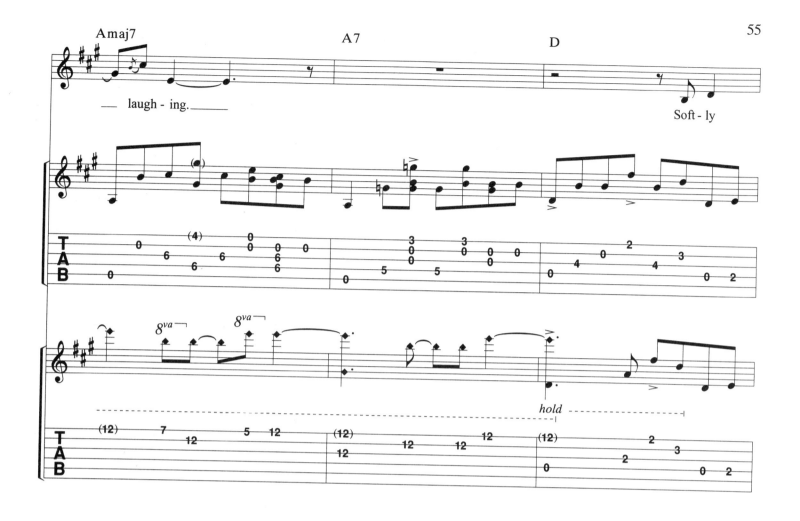

Down_ the dark - ened hall,_ I hear_ her foot - steps on my_ stair._

Then she is in_____ my arms once more._____

in the dawn._____

D.S. 𝄋 al Coda

Coda

Bridge:

Gtr. 1
Gtr. 2
(w/low mix ad lib.)

*Gtrs. 2 & 3

Softly - 5 - 4
PG9632

*Two gtrs. arranged for one.

Verse 2:
Softly she sighs.
Sweetly she lies, never sleeping.
Her fragrance all in my keeping.
Softly she comes in the night.

Verse 3:
Then softly she goes.
Her shining lips in the shadows
Whisper good-bye at my window.
Softly she goes in the dawn.

SONG FOR A WINTER'S NIGHT

(a/k/a The Hands I Love)

Words and Music by
GORDON LIGHTFOOT

Gtrs. 1 & 3 capo 2nd fret.
Gtr. 2 capo 7th fret.

* The number "5" in TAB represents
capoed open string.

Verses:

Gtr. 3
(Acoustic)

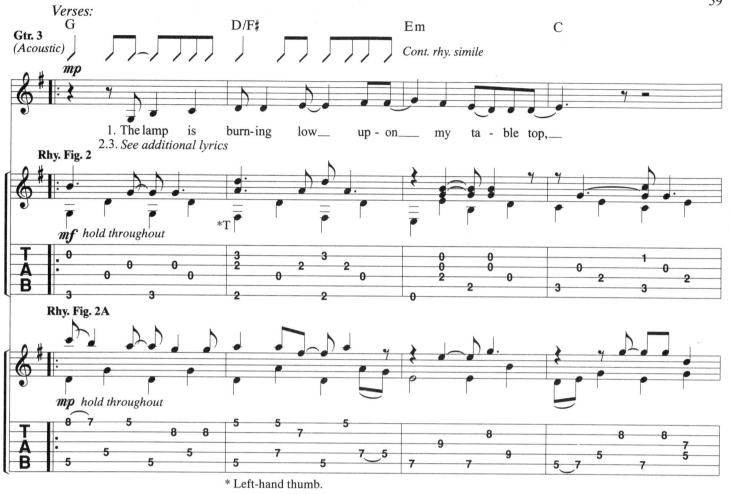

1. The lamp is burn-ing low___ up-on___ my ta-ble top,___
2.3. *See additional lyrics*

* Left-hand thumb.

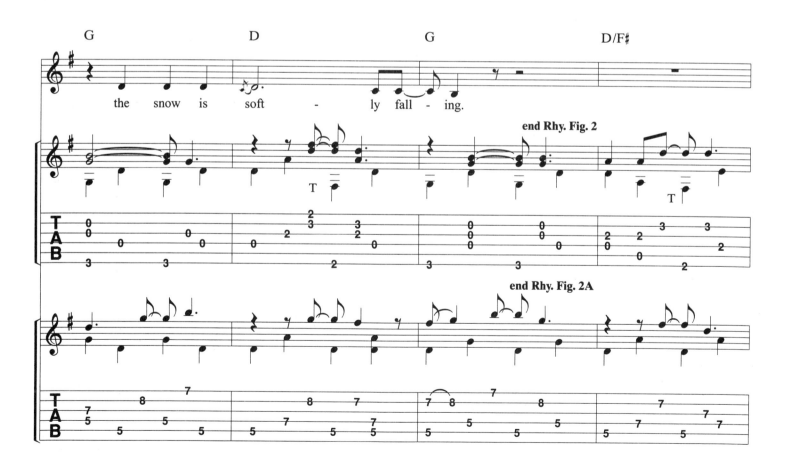

the snow is soft - ly fall - ing.

And to be once___ a - gain___ with___

Outro:
G

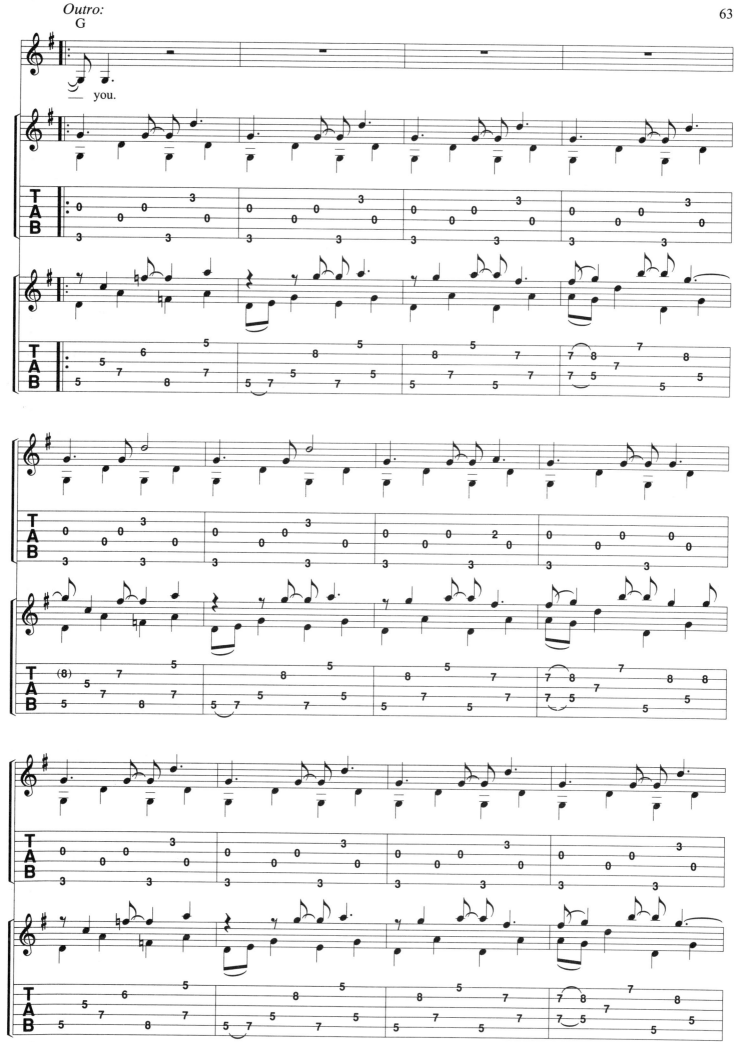

Repeat and fade
w/vcl. ad lib

Verse 2:
The smoke is rising in the shadows overhead,
My glass is almost empty.
I read again between the lines on the page,
The words of love you sent me.

Pre-Chorus:
If I could know within my heart
That you were lonely, too.

Verse 3:
The fire is dying now, my lamp is growing dim,
The shades of night are lifting.
The morning light steals across my windowpane,
Where webs of snow are drifting.

Pre-Chorus:
If I could only have you near,
To breathe a sigh or two.

STEEL RAIL BLUES

Gtr. 1 capo 1st fret.

Words and Music by
GORDON LIGHTFOOT

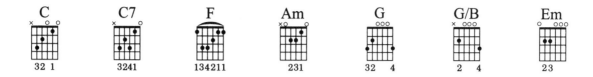

Moderate blues in 2 ♩ = 98

Intro:
C

Gtr. 1 *(Acoustic)*

mf hold throughout

1. Well, I

*Gtr. 2 *(Acoustic)*

mf

*Recorded w/capo 5 frets above Gtr. 1.
The 5th fret in tablature is the capoed open string.

Steel Rail Blues - 7 - 1
PG9632

%. *Verses:*

C

Gtr. 3 *(Acoustic 12-string)*

Cont. rhy. simile

Gtr. 4 *(Acoustic ad lib.)*

C7

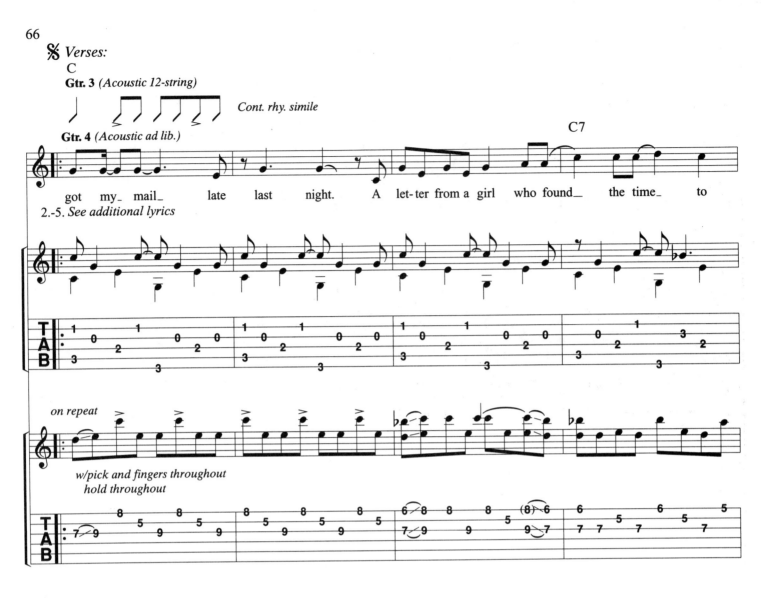

got my mail late last night. A let-ter from a girl who found the time to

2.-5. See additional lyrics

on repeat

w/pick and fingers throughout
hold throughout

F

C

write to her lone - some boy, some-where's in the night. She

mf

Steel Rail Blues - 7 - 3
PG9632

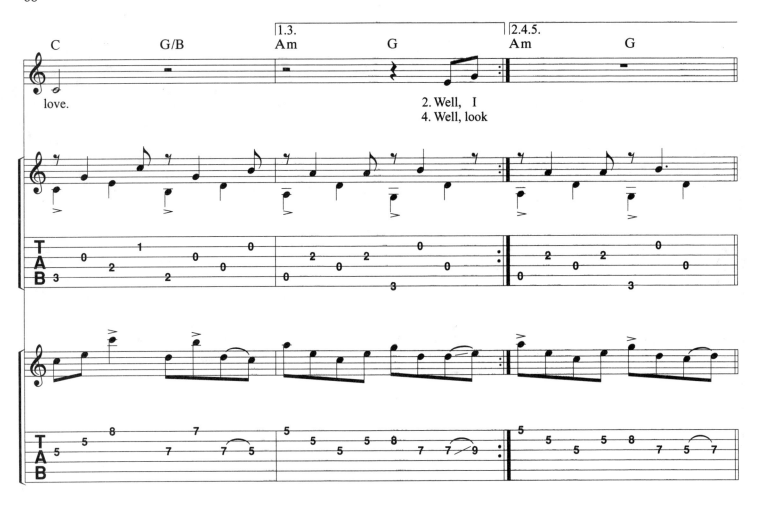

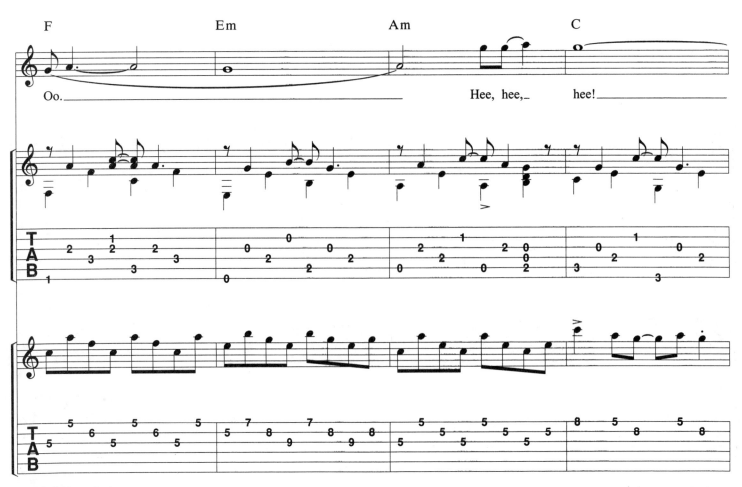

Steel Rail Blues - 7 - 4
PG9632

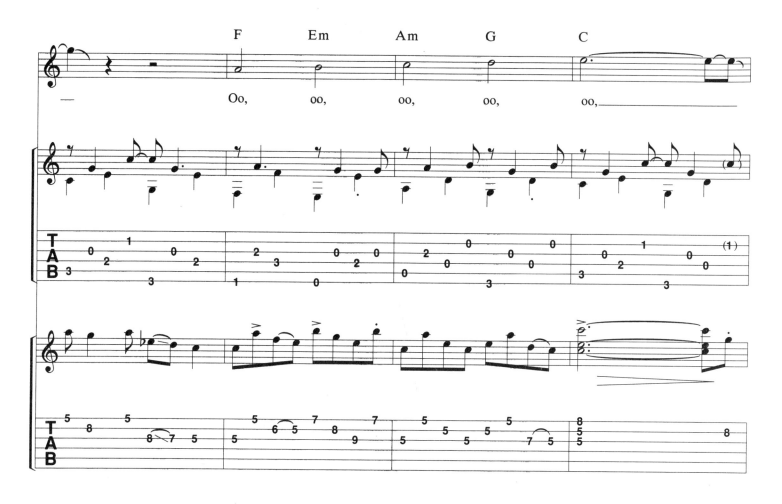

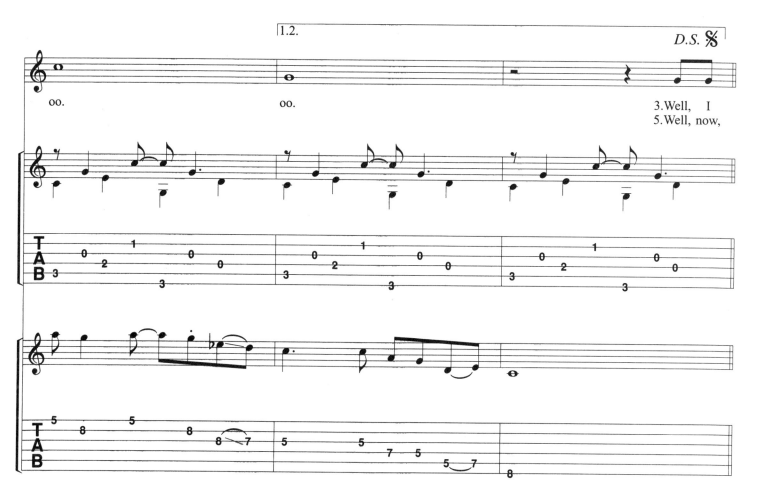

Steel Rail Blues - 7 - 5
PG9632

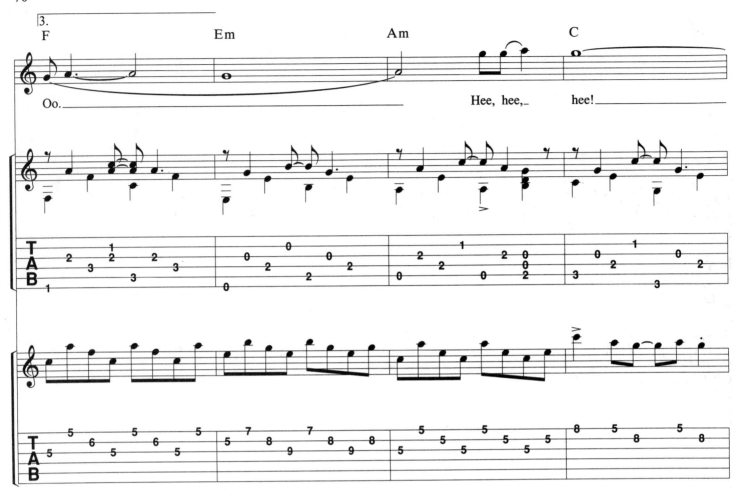

oo,   oo,   yik,   hee,___   hee.

Verse 2:
Well, I bin out here many long days.
I haven't found a place that I could call my own;
Not a two bit bed to lay my body on.
I bin stood up, I bin shook down,
I bin dragged into the sand.
And the big steel rail gonna carry me home
To the one I love.

Verse 3:
Well, I bin up tight most every night,
Walkin' along the streets of this old town,
Not a friend around to tell my troubles to.
My good old car, she done broke down,
'Cause I drove it into the ground.
And the big steel rail gonna carry me home
To the one I love.

Verse 4:
Well, I look over yonder across the plain.
The big drive wheels a-poundin' along the ground;
Gonna get on board and I'll be homeward bound.
Now, I ain't had a home cooked meal,
And Lord, I need one now.
And the big steel rail gonna carry me home
To the one I love.

Verse 5:
Now, here I am with my hat in my hand,
Standin' on the broad highway.
Would you give a ride to a lonesome boy who missed the train last night?
I went in town for one last round
And I gambled my ticket away,
And the big steel rail won't carry me home
To the one I love.

SUMMERTIME DREAM

**Words and Music by
GORDON LIGHTFOOT**

All gtrs. capo at 2nd fret.

Moderately in 2 ♩ = 98

74

Verse 4:

Guitar Solo:

D.S. 𝄋 al Coda

SUNDOWN

All gtrs. capo 2nd fret.

Words and Music by
GORDON LIGHTFOOT

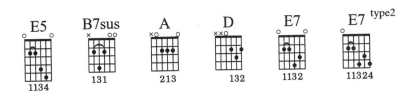

find___ you been creep - ing 'round___ my back___ stairs.___ Some - times I

think it's a sin___ when I feel like I'm win - ning, when I'm los - ing a - gain.___

Guitar Solo:

Cont. rhy. simile

Gtr. 3 *(Clean tone electric)*
Gtr. 2 *ad lib.*

w/Rhy. Fig. 1 *(Gtrs. 1 & 2) simile*

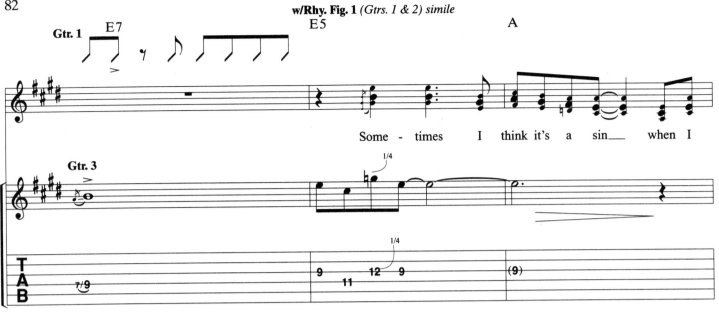

Some - times I think it's a sin___ when I

feel like I'm win-nin', when I'm los - in' a - gain.___

Outro:

Repeat and fade

THE WRECK OF THE EDMUND FITZGERALD

Words and Music by
GORDON LIGHTFOOT

The Wreck of the Edmund Fitzgerald - 7 - 3
PG9632

88

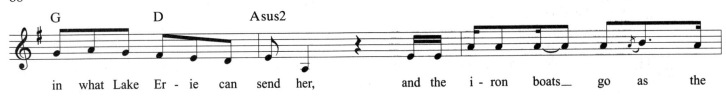

in what Lake Er - ie can send her, and the i - ron boats___ go as the

mar - i - ners all know, with the "Gales of No - vem - ber" re - mem - bered._____

w/Rhy. Fill 1 *(Gtr. 3) simile*

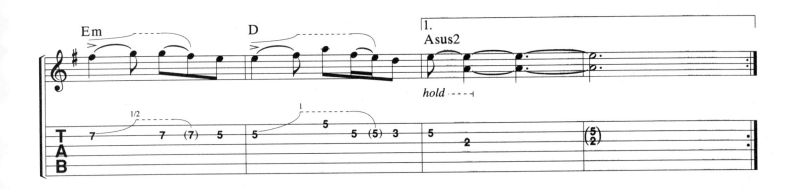

D.S. 𝄋 *al Coda*

7. In a

The Wreck of the Edmund Fitzgerald - 7 - 6
PG9632

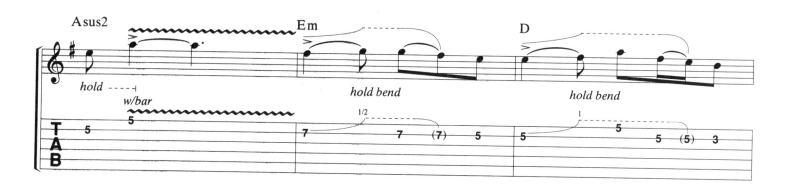

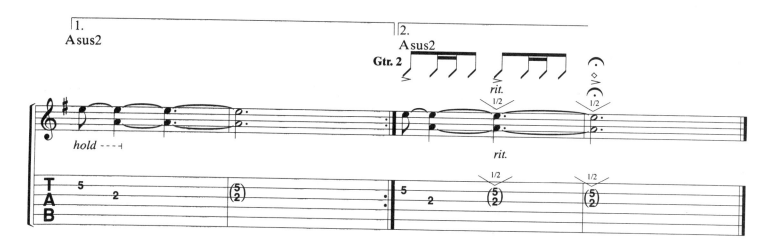

Verse 4:

When suppertime came, the old cook came on deck
Sayin', "Fellas, it's too rough to feed ya."
At seven p.m., a main hatchway caved in,
He said, "Fellas, it's bin good to know ya."
The captain wired in, he had water comin' in
And the good ship and crew was in peril.
And later that night, when 'is lights went out of sight,
Came the wreck of the Edmund Fitzgerald.

Verse 5:

Does anyone know where the love of God goes
When the waves turn the minutes to hours?
The searchers all say they'd have made Whitefish Bay
If they'd put fifteen more miles behind 'er.
They might have split up or they might have capsized,
They may have broke deep and took water.
And all that remains is the faces and the names
Of the wives and the sons and the daughters.

Verse 7:

In a musty old hall in Detroit, they prayed
In the maritime sailors' cathedral.
The church bell chimed 'til it rang 29 times
For each man on the Edmund Fitzgerald.
The legend lives on from the Chippewa on down
Of the big lake they called "Gitche Gumee."
Superior, they said, never gives up her dead
When the "Gales of November" come early.

(THAT'S WHAT YOU GET) FOR LOVIN' ME/
DID SHE MENTION MY NAME

All gtrs. capo 2nd fret.

Words and Music by
GORDON LIGHTFOOT

"(That's What You Get) For Lovin' Me"

Moderate country in 2 ♩ = 106

Verses:

1.4. That's what you get___ for lov-in' me.___
2.3. *See additional lyrics*

hold throughout

That's what you get___ for lov-in' me.___

(That's What You Get) For Lovin' Me - 10 - 2
PG9632

(That's What You Get) For Lovin' Me - 10 - 4
PG9632

"Did She Mention My Name"

Coda I   *Cont. rhy. simile*   *Verse 1:*

Chorus:

-tion___ my__ name___ just in___ pass - ing?___ And

when the morn - ing came,___ do you re - mem - ber if she dropped___

Verse 2:
w/Rhy. Fig. 1 (All gtrs.) simile

To Coda II

Guitar Solo:
w/Rhy. Fig. 1 (Gtrs. 1 & 3) 2 times, simile

98

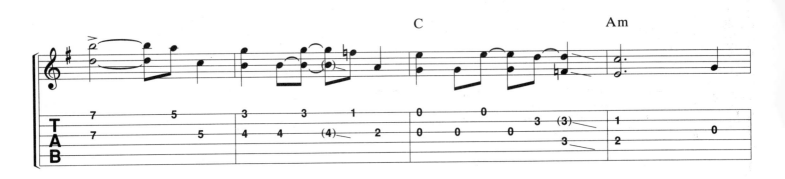

D.S. 𝄋𝄋 *al Coda II*

Did She Mention My Name - 10 - 9
PG9632

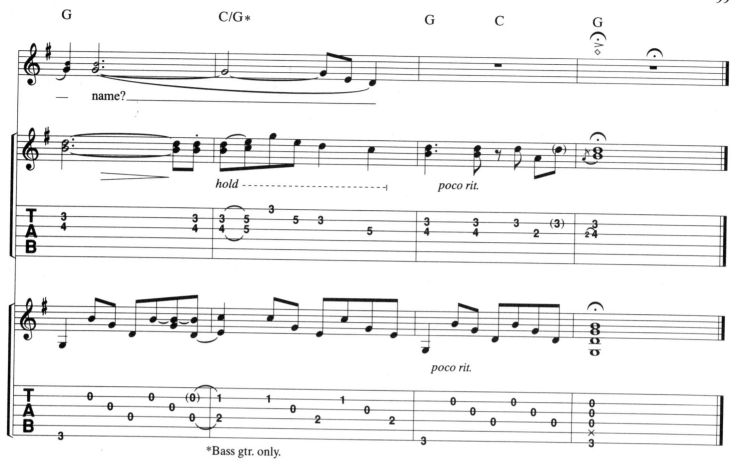

*Bass gtr. only.

(THAT'S WHAT YOU GET) FOR LOVIN' ME

Verse 2:
I ain't the kind to hang around
With any new love that I found.
Since movin' is my stock in trade.
I'm movin' on.
I won't think of you when I'm gone.

Verse 3:
So, don't you shed a tear for me
'Cause I ain't the love you thought I'd be.
I got a hundred more like you
So don't be blue.
I'll have a thousand 'fore I'm through.

DID SHE MENTION MY NAME

Chorus: (on D.S.)
Did she mention my name just in passing?
And when the talk ran high,
Did the look in her eyes seem far away?

Verse 4:
Won't you say hello from someone,
They'll be lonely to explain.
And by the way. . .

GUITAR TAB GLOSSARY **

TABLATURE EXPLANATION

READING TABLATURE: Tablature illustrates the six strings of the guitar. Notes and chords are indicated by the placement of fret numbers on a given string(s).

String ⑥, 3rd Fret   String ① 12th Fret   A "C" Chord   C Chord Arpeggiated
String ③ 13th Fret

BENDING NOTES

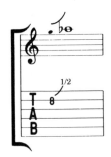

HALF STEP: Play the note and bend string one half step.*

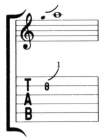

WHOLE STEP: Play the note and bend string one whole step.

PREBEND AND RELEASE: Bend the string, play it, then release to the original note.

RHYTHM SLASHES

STRUM INDICA-TIONS: Strum with indicated rhythm.

The chord voicings are found on the first page of the transcription underneath the song title.

INDICATING SINGLE NOTES USING RHYTHM SLASHES: Very often single notes are incorporated into a rhythm part. The note name is indicated above the rhythm slash with a fret number and a string indication.

*A half step is the smallest interval in Western music; it is equal to one fret. A whole step equals two frets.

**By Kenn Chipkin and Aaron Stang

ARTICULATIONS

HAMMER ON: Play lower note, then "hammer on" to higher note with another finger. Only the first note is attacked.

PULL OFF: Play higher note, then "pull off" to lower note with another finger. Only the first note is attacked.

LEGATO SLIDE: Play note and slide to the following note. (Only first note is attacked).

PALM MUTE: The note or notes are muted by the palm of the pick hand by lightly touching the string(s) near the bridge.

ACCENT: Notes or chords are to be played with added emphasis.

DOWN STROKES AND UPSTROKES: Notes or chords are to be played with either a downstroke (⊓) or upstroke (∨) of the pick.